The Green Lady

and

other poems

R. W. Jones

Grosvenor House
Publishing Limited

This book is published by
Grosvenor House Publishing Ltd
Link House
140 The Broadway, Tolworth, Surrey, KT6 7HT.
www.grosvenorhousepublishing.co.uk

This book is a work of fiction. Any resemblance to
people or events, past or present, is purely coincidental.

A CIP record for this book
is available from the British Library

ISBN 978-1-80381-931-0

THE GREEN LADY

A legend of Caerphilly castle

Risen mournful, lonely, early, while chill dawn was breaking pearly
She tiptoed ramparts grim and surly
Ere the castle cockerels spoke
Left her silken raiments gleaming o'er her bloated Baron, dreaming
Wore her gold hair loosely gleaming
And a modest, moss-green cloak.

Past the cullis, up, bestriding, far she travelled, weeping, riding
Where the silvered mists were sliding
Till the gallop lamed her mare.
Beside a glittering watercourse, with patient mien and gentle force
The outcast Jude restored her horse
Then, gentler still, healed her.

Pale sun smiled as mist withdrew. Magic limned his eyes, lake-blue
Tender, touched with sparkling dew
He drew her into light.
Milord, omniscient in his tower, with blandishments and martial power
Had claimed her hand, outlaid the dower
And raped her wedding night.

Jude's cheek was scarred, his hands, nut-brown yet delicate as thistledown
Unfurled her on the moss-green gown
Beneath leaves fresh and shady
He quickened sweetly to her flood, redeemed her wounded womanhood
Two souls, two hearts, two lives, one blood
The Outcast and his lady.

So began their starlit mission, secret passion, ardent kissing
Stolen fruit, forbidden trysting
Till the Baron learned his name.
Chained her to high tower casing, naked, shorn and outward facing
Her reawaken bloom debasing
Forcing all to see her shame.

Nightfall. A horned moon beclouded. Ghosting through grey sentries crowded
In stealth and rescue-rope enshrouded
Jude scaled the bleak black stone
Moonshafts through the cloudlace breaching lit her chill flesh, bare and bleaching
Lit her chained hands, pale, beseeching
Lit them stark in monochrome

The squat Baron, leering under, set the fuse and sparked the thunder
Crimson ripped the walls asunder
Seared them into martyrhood
For minstrels sang in secret rhyme of how their broken forms reclined

They fell as lovers, intertwined
Two souls, two hearts, one blood

Stout-walled, the ancient castle stands, oft-restored and long unmanned
Daylight paints it bold but bland
Yet no-one can explain
How sometimes in the cold moon gleaming, through the shattered tower leaning
Ghosts a lady, green and keening
Whispering Jude's name.

TO J D – A CONTRADICTION

A famous poet once wrote
That no man is an island. But he
Was wrong. For I am an island.
I am an island in the restless sea of humanity
Whose storms and waves and undertows
Beat heavy on the sturdy reef of indifference
Amassed from lifelong grains of cynic coral
That guards my sandy, vulnerable shore.
I am an island
Standing bare against the greedy tides
Whose stealthy violence threatens to engulf me.
Is this heroic? No, you say. Just stupid.
But if, some balmy day I should allow
Those lulling, wooing waters to encroach
Then I become
Simply another droplet in that same sea
Whose swirling currents press me where
I do not want to go.
A friend once told me
That war is immoral, that the only thing
Worth fighting for is peace; and we only
Fight for peace by refusing to fight
And I, being young, believed his shining
Circle of logic. But I now see

That there are other causes worthy of my death
And thus worth fighting for. And if
I will not fight, then why should others?
I will not fight for glory or an empty politician's word.
But fight I must. Because I clearly see
That when my fleeting sprint through life is done
And I, breathless, stagger to the tape, I shall
In those final seconds, stand alone
Afraid
And face myself.

And you, my love, who by
Your strong trust and beauty
Broke down the reef and swim in my lagoon
Even you, who sometimes touch the shore
Can never reach the secrets of the isle
I do not know them all myself.
And if we both may lie like twin atolls,
The water in between, though calm, is deep.
Only the steady silt of enjoined years
Can build the narrow causeway
And link your next-door island to mine
This, too, is brief, for in the dying seaquake
That swallows up our causeway, and drowns us both
You too, must stand alone and search your soul
And answer, yes or no. Therefore,
I am an island.

ICE MAIDEN

Whitest of angels, from a leaden sky
Descending muffled, stealthily you go
Sparkling death and frozen wonder ply
Smothering, frost-fluffed eiderdown of snow.

See iced confetti o'er the landscape's face
Winging in silence down a wintry aisle
You wed your pallid virtue with due grace
To Father Earth, who does your robe defile

Virginal cherub, to the altar bring
'Neath unsoiled raiment, chillingly serene
Promise of cold delights and claim your king
And spread your lifeless white above his green

Yet though exhausted, pale and still, he lives
Though cruel your bite, though deep the pain be felt
Dawn heralds warmth, and warmth new courage gives
Even your glacial heart must yield – and melt

A LAMENT FOR LOCKDOWN

(Sung to the tune of the 12 days of Christmas)

On the first day of lockdown my truelove sent to me

A photo of Tesco's, empty

On the second day.........sent to me   2 deserted diners

On the third day.......sent to me   3 silent pubs

On the fourth day.......sent to me   4 curfewed cafes

On the fifth day........sent to me   5 crippled cruise ships

On the sixth day.......sent to me   6 panicked punters

On the seventh day.......sent to me 7 growing graveyards

On the eighth day.......sent to me 8 abandoned airfields

On the ninth day........sent to me   9 knackered nurses

On the tenth day........sent to me 10 testing tubes

On the eleventh day.......sent to me 11 early exits

On the twelfth day.......sent to me 12 trendy tombs

Nothing like a bit of black humour when things are tough.

22nd March 2020

PANDEMIC POSER

Pray doctor, your wisdom impart

A family we're anxious to start

So kindly prescribe

How we further our tribe

Whilst remaining two metres apart

PANDEM-MANIA

In days gone by, just thieves and surgeons went to work in masks
And coffin makers took their time to fashion fancy casks
Back then, the height of hitech was a rooftop tv dish
The net was something that held hair or sometimes caught you fish
Then from deepest USA the word began to spread
No need for wires or letters, there was world wide web instead
Ever onward, ever upward from the tropics to the poles
We had email, movie streaming, social media – and trolls.
Unwitting, unsuspecting, we sailed serenely on
Homo sapiens ascending, what could possibly go wrong?
Yet unbeknown and unforeseen within the far-off East
Something stirred, a tiny, bloodless, terrifying beast
No-one alive could touch it, taste or smell or see or hear it.
At first, entrenched in hubris, we were too obtuse to fear it.
So now amidst intensive care and haunted by mass graves
We cower behind bolted doors in stark, locked-down enclaves
And wonder, are we near the final fatal downward spiral
That will bring a whole new meaning to the common phrase – gone viral

THE ELEMENTS

1.   WATER – the stream of consciousness

Out of a loving blood-warm reservoir

Sprung gently to the brittle light of day

Trickling shallow through my infant mind;

Seeking, arrow-straight and diamond clear

Between the mossy-cushioned banks of youth

A simple, callow, superficial brook

Of adolescent thought.

Deepening, clouded with the sediment of years

In the tidal swelling of my manhood stream

Flowing, lusty to the troubled sea;

It lives awhile midst raging, storm-tossed waves

Touched by secret undertows unknown to even me

And later, whirlpools down the last, long

Salty eddying vortex that sucks me, pitiless

Through swift senility and loveless death

Forever.

2.   FIRE – the flame of inspiration

Kindled in childish innocence

Sparked on a sun-dried twig of unseen light

Burning cool until one waking dawn;

A blazing vision blinds the startled eye

And bids the questing, unformed mind to strive

Groping for unknown words to name

An unnameable pain

And ever since this moment, growing strong
Fed on Nature's dark and grimy coal
Flaming hatred down the smoky years
It briefly flares beneath a sooted pall
That chokes those same bright torches till they fade
Into weary, flickering candle of disinterest
Swaying sadly, drained of vital warmth
A failing ember, winking out
Forever.

3.   EARTH – the dust of the flesh
Conceived one early, dew-spread morn
Sprung from a buried root of earthly joy
Carried deep within the vaulted womb:
The fresh-sown seed grows quick and softly swells
Searching, blind beneath the comforting soil
Bursting slender into pale spring sun
To stand uneasy.
Swayed by the wafting wind of heedless youth
Whose lightest breath demands a humble bow
It flowers boldly in the Summer warmth
And casts a cape of colour in the cave:
Then fades at Autumn's first ice-fingered touch
Withered, frozen, spent, and lying naked
On the winter's frosty couch of earth to rot
Lost to the quickening sun
Forever.

THE RISING SUN

Written when grants were used to attract foreign investors to the valleys

The rising sun brings little warmth
A dead man lies underneath by here
No Rest In Peace for him as blind white worms will nuzzle
And the slow rot of time will melt his flesh
While stone angels make a perch for crows above his head
He worked curled to a question mark
Half a mile below, with only pale eye sockets
To mark his face apart
From the cold black, old black face of coal.

The earth rang like struck skin
On some dark God's great drum.
A pit-prop squealed. He died at once
Snuffed out by fallen rock, his mouth a silent scream
His eyewhites bulging like small moons.
As we approached the shaft coughed dust and swallowed him.

We told his wife in starlight beneath the winding wheel
Her cheekbones taut and jutting, a baby daughter dozing in her arms
Fetch him up, she pleaded, Give him Christian dues
Nobody knew how.

He came from war a scarecrow
In clothes that billowed round him like a shroud
The Burmah Railway had him, hot green jungle, leeches
Brutal little yellow folk. He hated Japanese men
Even more than Coal Board bosses.
Angharad saved him; her dark-haired plainness blossomed
Every time he spoke
To see him with her and that girlchild
Held so tender in his coal-scarred hands
Was to see a man redeemed
Till the dark drum struck, and he was gone.

Somewhere in London, with slashes of his pen
A coal Board boss destroyed our pit
Uneconomic, he wrote, too costly to maintain.
I stand in early sunshine and remember Idwal
Crushed these thirty years
Curved into a question mark, his ribrack
Making imprints in cold shale
He'll be a fossil one day.
They cut the winding wheel away with harsh bright flame
And smashed the pit-head buildings down
Tips are growing over by this fancy factory
With plate glass windows and blue walls
No men work among the daffodils
Of this new greened valley. This factory's for women.

Idwal's daughter comes here every day
She works in white, masked like a surgeon
Her neat, sweet fingers plating tiny metal parts
Behind a screen that's greener than her eyes
So is Idwal grinning in his cold, cramped crypt?
Does his spirit smile, somewhere below?
No, and I am seething when I see the reason why

A big car draws up, quiet as a cloud
He steps out and the glass doors sigh apart for him
He's short, with seal-sleek dark hair
Sunshine splinters on his pebble spectacles
He owns us now. His name is
Isiguro Tagasaki.

ODES TO JILL

I write this as I'm leaving so you'll know
This time and every other time I go
My heart will stay with you while I'm away
And I'll love you every hour, every day.

Way back when we were young
I thought I couldn't love you more
Relentless time grinds on
And leaves me feeling not so sure
Though faculties decline
As we approach the latter stage
I see that, like the finest wine
Great love improves with age.

However stark the journey
However dark the night
As long as you walk with me
There will be love – and light

ELECTION MEDLEY

Click goes the TV, click click click
No matter what the channel is it makes you parrot sick
Some are rough and ornery, some are smooth and slick
But every one's a shyster and a bloody polly tick

Gallop dropped a rowlock
Harris should have stuck to tweed
The NOP had Labour on a roll
Auntie MORI told a story
There wasn't any need
Everybody knows they're up the poll

All the local pundits gathered in the pub
Tory, Labour, Plaid and Liberal D
Hung parliament, they muttered, there's the rub
What's it going to mean to you and me?
The landlord set his pint down and eyed them one by one
Then delivered judgement, loud and slow
Hung parliament? He bellowed, without a trace of fun
We shoulda done it long ago

ELEGY FOR A GODFATHER

This tribute comes from we who call ourselves the Welsh connexion

From ancient vales and hills where Don was held in huge affection

In view of his profession he would naturally belong

A mellow, modern minstrel in our fabled Land of Song

A man of many talents, a star of stage and show

The fact that Lesley loved him tells you all you need to know

We were sadly never able to enjoy him in his prime

But are privileged and grateful to have shared a little time

As a travelling companion, he proved, to no surprise

Generous, compassionate, funny, warm and wise

The senior among us, he was always number one

The stewards all deferred to him – the Godfather, don Don

The name belied his nature, ever courteous, ever calm

And few indeed were those who failed to recognise his charm

Our final voyage together threw up obstacles to face

Harsh injury and illness borne with humour, grit and grace

He's free from pain and anguish now and though we're all bereft

We've precious, treasured memories to fill the void he's left

Our last farewell we borrow from the Bard, who says it best

"Good night, sweet prince, may choirs of angels sing thee to thy rest"

LEIGH'S ELEGY

My great regret, Leigh told me once, when times were not so fraught
I might have been a giant but my legs were too damn short.
This quote begins my tribute, I've chosen it because
It demonstrates precisely the kind of man he was
Cheerful and resilient in sickness and in health
And always quite prepared to take the mickey from himself
Down to earth and practical, entirely without guile
A wicked sense of humour and a warm, infectious smile
He relished his position at the Basset family's head
He loved his wife, his children, his grandkids – and his shed.
For that was where so many broken, treasured things were sent
If Leighton said he'd mend them, then trust me – they got ment
So now with poignant irony it grieves me to report
Exactly like those legs he blamed, his life was too damn short.
If you think I've been facetious, please don't let it make you cross
It's just my way of trying to soften this great loss
For though the mood be sombre, though our eyes be damp and dim
We're all a little better for the gift of knowing him

A LAMENT OF LOVE AND LUCK

Sadly and silently walked my Lord
In a coach on the northbound train
In time with the judder and clank of the wheels
Which kindled dull sparks in his brain
With hands numb and cold he fingered the gold
Which mournfully clinked at his side
And he thought long and hard on the turn of the card
That had cost him his soon-to-be bride

Creamy and fair was his Rosemary Gay
A woman of ignoble birth
Whose father sold second hand sewing machines
With faint hope of reward on this earth.
He had met her one day on Chancery Way
And her smile had illumined the gloom
So taking her arm, with panache and with charm
He invited her back to his room.

Of course she declined this audacious approach
Though obviously not too displeased
So he persisted, he begged and cajoled
Until Rosemary weakened, appeased
In the weeks that ensued, he ardently wooed
This maiden of delicate grace
She seemed to enjoy each flattering ploy
And their courtship proceeded apace

But when he repaired to the family abode
To offer her up for inspection
His mater and pater, in no way impressed
Emphatically plumped for rejection
Undaunted though sad, they flew to *her* Dad
And met with a second disaster
He cried "Don't come back, because blue blood I lack
And I won't have a Lord as her master."

Still, young love can stand such reverses as these
And they rented a sinful apartment
Which they shared with an artist of dubious means
And a clerk from the Sewage department
For a while problems eased and they did as they pleased
On the strength of his bountiful credit
But before many days she tired of such ways
And existence in permanent debit.

One evening, by way of reviving their joy
They entered an upmarket nightclub
Where the atmosphere suited her down to the ground
Though he reckoned it wasn't the "right" club
On a table nearby, he chanced to espy

A very high stakes game of Chemmy
He said "Sit and sup while I go and clean up
I'll coin us a right pretty penny."

He entered the fray in the midst of a lull
And the bank stood well-covered and stable
But "Banco!" he cried, in the rashness of youth
And a hush settled over the table
They played. He went down by five hundred pounds
"Let's go double or quits," said his Lordship.
"I'll give it a whirl if you put up your girl."
"Right. Done." Twas the end of their courtship.

The cards were faced up – but need I say more?
He lost by a singular number
She left him, unmoved, for she knew but too well
What men join they may easily sunder
And now when they meet on Carnaby Street
She smiles, on the arm of her banker
While he ruefully grins; for the price of his sins
He's wed Lady Ffortesque-Planker

SQUIDOODLE

Buy a sacred icon? breathed Del Carrot to Le Squid
White platinum, gold wire and a steal at fifteen quid?
Pardonnez, mon petit chou, quoth the Gallic cephalopod
I 'ave not a single mange tout and I don't believe in God
We could do it never never, the vegetable decreed
APR the lowest ever, satisfaction guaranteed
'As it fallen off a dinghy? queried Squid, all innocence
Grated Carrot, OK stingy, just for you it's eighty pence.

A passing Spanish Mackerel murmured hola, bless my sole
Zis poor Parisian tentacle will end up on the dole
He circumtoured Bermuda, danced flamenco on slick fins
Drumming up two barracuda and a school of terrapins
Hasta, bueno amigos, he chuntered as they swum
We shall storm archipelagos for our down-trod, ten-armed chum!
They followed, young fish, old fish, shrimp, manatee and whale
Sprat, wrasse and even goldfish to the submarine boot sale.

Meanwhile, sick as Flaubert's Parrot from selling at a loss
The calumniferous Carrot starting arguing the toss
Saying try to shangrilar me, you translucent milquetoast
And you'll end up calamari, buttered, battered sliced and roast.
Diable, Le Squid hooted, c'est un outrage, c'est le Guerre

I 'ate plants that's rooted, specially with ginger 'air!
Warned Del Carrot – Octopuplet, draw your final froggy breath
Squid squared off – in quintutuplet – and began the dance of death

Terrapupils all quit writing times tables on their slates
El Mackerel turned whiting, pouting shadly, smuggling skates
Wrasse wrestled, 'cudas coodled, many manatees made sure
That every sprat's sprog oodled to the Great Squid-Carrot war.
It didn't take a twinkling. reef-roofs rippled with pink pulp
Squid squoze out every inkling, downing Carrot in one gulp
Since then all creatures finny know two truths, clear and sharp
Every carrot's red and skinny and squids see in the dark.

FIRESIDE CONVERSATION

Written during years of working in Kenya

We sat, replete, beside the spicy embers
Of a eucalyptus fire that was a small oasis
In the velvety, soot-sanded desert of African night.
Leaning idle, tracing shapeless patterns
In the fine red talcum powder dust, I asked,
For want of something else to say
"What are your thoughts, O father?"
The firelight's fleeting fingers etched a living cast of shadows
On the noble, time-eroded features of dull-sheened anthracite,
And he replied "I think of supper. It was good. And of the crops.
They promise well. But mostly, I wonder on your
Countryman, who calls himself a Missionary"
"Old Ronnie? Then let us talk of him awhile.
What does the voice within your head say of him?"
"He is a strange man. A fierce man to preach
The ways of peace. Truly, he heals our sickening children,
Bathes our scratches, aids us on our lands,
But when a man who passes his house
Bears off a paw-paw, or beats his wife for idleness
Or drinks a magic potion to ease an ache,
Why then his pale face darkens to the
Shade of oxen's blood and he shouts and rages,

Stuttering of sin. And when our women
Walk unclothed in innocence, he frowns and sulks.
Does he not know, fruits which are forbidden taste the sweeter?
And when the warring tribesmen from the West
Steal in and take our cattle from the pen
And we in anger, answer with our spears
He calls us wicked, saying we must not fight.
O you of understanding, explain to me.
What is his demon?"
Unthinking, weighing not my speech, I answered lightly
"He loves the word of God."
A sly hyena, listening, assayed an insane giggle
And swiftly seizing on my carelessness
The old man said "Whose God? Not ours.
Our God is mighty. Should we leave his paths
He strikes at us with plague and drought and hunger
And if a man should kill, he dies.
And if he steals a cow, his own will die
And if he takes another's wife, his own lies barren.
What of your God and his only son
That the Missionary so loves?"
"Of God, I know but little, of Jesus, more.
He was a man, born to earth who lived
To cast his steady, inextinguishable glow of love
Into an age dark with war and hate.
He loved the world and all within it. He turned the other cheek."

"So tell me, clever one," he said, gently ironic, "What became of him?"
"You know it well enough. His people killed him."
"Ah. A just reward. Attend me well;
If my dog displeases me and I take a stick
And beat him till my anger dies and throw the stick away
That same dog uncurls his drooping tail
And, bounding off, brings back the stick
That I may beat some more. Yet, if I,
While hunting leopard, throw my spear too lightly
And only wound, does the beast return it to me?
No. He leaps and kills me, lest I should kill him first.
Therefore, I love the dog, but I respect the leopard."
"But father, which of these two, respect or love, is nobler?"
"My son, a man may respect without loving
But he cannot truly love without respecting."
A cricket cheered. The hidden trees
Whispered their agreement to this fundamental truth.
The old man said "We were talking of your friend.
Why did he come?"
"He came to bring the Word, to show the way."
"The word of love?" "None else."
"My son, the word is wrong. My tribe
Is deaf to love. The only word that flushes out
Their waxy ears and bids them hear is Freedom."
"Indeed? And what is this freedom?"
"Freedom is a shiny motor car.

Freedom is a mobile telephone with websites.
Freedom is a fatted buffalo that every day walks gladly to
An idle knife and sticks himself
And skins himself and lies within the pot
So all we have to do is eat his meat. Or so the politicians say.
And we believe, because we wish it so.
Your friend has come an age too soon.
We do not understand his truth.
In teaching, he confuses. In his life
He angers us. He tears away the temples of tradition
Building instead a fragile hut of grass that sways and bends
And falls before the first breath of disagreement.
Lacking foundation in our history.
The Children who among us heed his words
Are outcasts, little black men acting white.
It seems he wants to wipe away our past
And build a future which denies all
Our ancient culture. Why, then does he stay?"
"He stays because he loves both you, and God."
The fire died. A distant lion coughed.
The old man stirred and sighed, a sound
Of weary patience from another age.
"Then we shall listen, silent
And forgive him."

THE BALLAD OF ST. VALENTINE

Or how the test was won.

Young Val, he was a cricketer, a handsome, lusty rover
And forceful was the arm with which he bowled the maidens over
King Hector was his sovereign liege, and had a buxom daughter
Whom he was loathe to marry off, though wise men said he oughta.
Her given name was Mary-Ann, her old man called her Nancy
And Val forsook his errant ways when Nancy caught his fancy
Alas, poor lad, he was low born, his love went unrequited
Before she'd share come-hither looks he'd have to be beknighted.

And thus the matter might have stood till fate put in a hand
A strident challenge from abroad was heard throughout the land.
Bold Baron Botham dwelt next door, a castle 'cross the water
He yearned to ravish hector's corn – and also, Hector's daughter.
One morning in the month of May, with silver bugles pealing
He crossed the dyke and set up stumps on Hector's cricket fielding.
"Ho varlet" quoth the mighty Both, "let's have a wager, sporting!
I'm in the mood to raise a brood but can't abide the courting."

"Trot out thy knaves and bowling men and set up thy pavilion
If thou can'st knock my wicket down I'll pay thee half a million.
Mark what I say, by close of play, if stumps remain intactus
Then thou shalt pledge me Mary-Ann and never more contact us."

Now Hector's stores stood fearful low, his coffers sore depleted
And so he knew, by hook or crook, that Both must be defeated.
And though he held his daughter dear, his brain was all a-whirling
With dreams of jewels and indoor pools and half a million, sterling.

King Hector summoned up his team of speedy men and seamers
And bade them mix a devil's brew of cutters, spin and beamers.
"Wear him down," a sage advised "Until he's proper flakers
Then sling a fast one at his box and give him two new acres"
The valiant knights toiled through the day, their language ever warmer.
Ever tried to skittle Both whilst wearing full dress armour?
The Baron smote them far and yon, his footwork light and dainty
Some muttered "'Tis a sorcerer," Quoth Val "Let's do it quaintly."

Till at last as night drew nigh and Mary-Ann lay weeping
Young Val rose up and promised her "I'll give him wicket keeping!"
"O noble churl, please save the girl, and if you so delight me
And bowl out Both, then by my troth I surely shall beknight thee."
Neath setting sun, off his shorter run, Young Val produced a corker
It moved from leg to middle peg, Ye Olde Worlde yorker
A hapless flail, a flying bail, Both gaped in stupefaction
"No ball!" cried he "For all can see, he hath a suspect action!"

"Bad loser!" cried the joyous King "Thou art a batting failure!"
And Botham gagged, and packed his bags, and slunk off to Australia.
The king took up his sword and cried "You saved this gal 'o mine,

And won the test, thy name be blessed, arise, St Valentine!"
The moral of this story is, to win a girl, or cup
In love be true and while you do, keep all your balls well up.
And this is why when Spring steals through in hedgerow, copse and thicket
A young man's fancy lightly turns to dalliance – and cricket.

A DIGRESSIONARY ODE

(*Variations on a theme of Mrs G A Jones*)
Corona was a beer – it's now become a virus
How do such common words manage to inspire us?
When we were striplings Corona stood for pop
Pop goes the weasel.
When you say weasel what others come to mind
Ferrets, or creatures of the polecat kind?
Taffy never thinks that way, mind you
Begging your pardon, Taffy who?
Never mind.
He might well say the virus makes you dead, see
Very salty water, Dead Sea.
What happens when salty water comes to mind?
Water on the brain
Encephalitis.
And whenever such harsh pandemics start to spread
You simply can't keep medi-jargon out of your head
Never forget
Elephantiasis,
The genesis for this all derives from Jill
When it comes to rhyming, she's a tigress
Ah, but I digress

March 2020

COLD BLOOD

They crossed in cleric's collars as daybreak sidled in
Bearing altar candles and a panoply of sin
They made covert communion, hunched like cellar rats
Breathing terror's incense, sieving death from molten wax
Beneath a high rise Temple where concrete caged the light
They buried desecration in an obscene, furtive rite

Sing rebel songs to greet them
For no matter what they do
Irregulars are heroes
Their cause is just and true.

She drifted through the drizzle in an evening gown of jade
Enchanted by the echoes of First Night accolade
She was innocent of malice, bigotry or spite
Bright-eyed and golden-headed, savouring the night
Street-neon limned her beauty, making jewel-strings of the rain
The fireball slashed her, shrieking, in a razor-blaze of pain.

Pluck glass-shards from her eyeballs
Rinse her cold blood from the dust
Then ask her bereft parents
If the cause is true or just.

JOYRIDE

Freaky Evans cut classes at quarter to two
Hot-wired a Porsche at ten past
Snorted coke with a chaser of acetate glue
Gave himself and the engine a blast
Twin exhausts bellowed thunder to quicken his blood
Death was a sleek, silver squeal
With two hundred horsepower under the hood
And twelve-year old hands at the wheel

Pre-nursery school toddlers were crossing the lane
The Porsche tossed them skyward like chaff
They sprawled, smeared in scarlet, keening and maimed
Because Freaky "just wanted a laugh."
Shattered limbs, doll-like corpses cut off at the neck
Whey-faced paramedics struck dumb
Freaky walked free from the blood-spattered wreck
Bemoaning a lightly bruised thumb.

He's parentless, pitiless, too young to gaol
What use prattle of "sparing the rod?"
If you're burning for justice and right to prevail
Don't ask Freaky Evans. Ask God.

NEW PENGAM - A CAUTIONARY ODE

Written after a brand new school build opened

Farewell to thee, old Pengam, thy days are dead and gone
Bad memories are fading, the good ones linger on.
Amazing that we made it through all those barren years
Some laced with loony laughter, most torn with tortured tears.
With half stuck down at Gradfa, and the rest in Pengam set
Traipsing over layered litter, past graffiti, in the wet.
Mornings in a Chem lab rendered dim by twisted trees
It was no use quaffing coffee; you needed anti-freeze.
Assemblies in the chapel where the dumbstruck organ stood
Bone-chilled yet oddly bonded, a benighted brotherhood.
Few teachers claimed a single room to nurture as a base
Trudging, book-encumbered, gypsy-like, from place to place
Few boys could be expected to observe the Golden Rule
Or venture forth enamoured of this fallen, once-great school.
Despite it all, we managed as each dismal day crawled by
The philosophy was simple – if we didn't laugh, we'd cry.

All this is now behind us; a bright new era dawns
Enshrined in fresh-set concrete, shiny steel and verdant lawns.
We have interactive whiteboards, drama studios, full IT
A salubrious sports hall, a palatial place to pee.

Yet reservations hover: as the poet wrote of old
Not all that shines is silver, nor all that glisters, gold.
Though most of you have manners worthy of applause
A few rip doors off lockers and defecate on floors.
Sadly, though the many may be wholly without blame
It only takes that feckless few to ruin our good name.
Do we really want folk saying –"They spent seven million quids
And it **is** a brilliant building – such a shame about the kids?"
OK, here's the crucial question – just what are we to do?
Sorry, I can't comment. That answer's down to **you.**
One thing I **can** tell you, without the smallest doubt
It's people that make places, not the other way about.

#

WHENWEES

Written on revisiting Kenya

It took your recent clever lays
With haunting beat and scan
To bring to mind those lovely days
And that unlovely man.
The future seemed awash with sun
The promise clear and bright
With plenty there for everyone
Though black or brown or white.
Who would have guessed when Mzee died
It would so quickly fade
And that a new-born nation's pride
Would be so oft betrayed?
They had the land, they had the Game
They had the clear intent
To wipe away historic shame
In that dark continent.
With bounty blessed, from hunger freed
And little left to dread
It only took a tyrant's greed
To turn it on it's head.

Or is it only we who see
A dim, half empty glass
And mourn for what can never be
As fine as times long past?
Like you I can but sadly dream
Good times may come again
But doubt that things will ever seem
As sweet as way back, when.

SOMETIMES

Sometimes, when winter wind stings salt tears to my eyes
My vision blurs and I remember her.
Sometimes when toothed blue embers gnaw the hearth
The flames unfurl and form her face.
A slim face, green-eyed and framed in chestnut hair
An ordinary face.
Then, on a sunset mountain while larks hung, blazing, over brassy tips
She turned; a look that went beyond keyed nerves and quickened blood
To stillness at the centre of our souls.
Her face had radiance I still close my eyes and see
And was never ordinary again.
Sometimes that summer as we trod silvered slopes
The stars seemed close enough to touch
Softly, surely, she spoke of life to come
The home we'd build, the love we'd share
The children we would raise

Things were different then. We daren't embrace, mouths mingled
Taut flesh urgent for release, which, too freely granted is
Too easily demeaned. We longed for oneness we could only know
In private and the blessing of our God.

When winter clothed the tips in white she took my hand
We'll marry in the Spring, she said. Wind stirred her hair.
Joy lit her eyes. Though black ice crunched beneath my boots

She warmed me like the sun.
Fever took her later that same week. No-one could reach her for the snow.
They told me when I came off shift. To this day
I don't remember who they were.
Don't weep, they said, she's gone into His grace. I wept
Because she'd gone from me. They covered her in virgin snow
And cold black earth. Abide With Me, they sang.
She always has.

Thirty years I've fought the coal and trudged these hills
And watched this quiet hearth alone. Women pleasured me
Some tender as a rose; but not to touch the stillness at my core.
Her voice still echoes deep in cold black earth, her face still beckons from the
flame.
Salt tears still burn for her and all I lost
Sometimes, in the winter wind.

TENDING THE FLAME – FOR GILLIAN

Once when the world and we were young, on a warm and moonlit hill

A small spark sprang between us – the flame burns strongly still

We were little more than children, puppy love, the doubters claimed

Even then we both knew better, knew enough to tend the flame

Faced with years apart in College, doubters said we'd drift away

But we kept the embers glowing with a letter every day

In an attic by a sunlit sea, at long last man and wife

We'd been in love since schooldays, we were lovers now for life

With my body I thee worship, so the marriage vow proclaimed

We joyfully embraced it, kept the faith and fanned the flame

Early years in vibrant Kenya were illumined with delight

The wonders of the daytime and the glories of the night

Dancing lampglow on your body and the images it gave

Are emblazoned on my memory, I'll take them to my grave

So began an idyll, worlds to conquer, dreams to share

We revelled in the newness and each other, free as air

Until, from sudden darkness came a savage, tragic pain

We could but cling together, mourn our loss and tend the flame

Slowly, very slowly, we emerged to clearer skies

Until a healthy newborn boy restored light to your eyes

A lovely girl soon followed and our cup welled to the brim

But fate had one more blow to strike, malevolent and grim

Once more the dark clouds lowered, we could find no-one to blame

Once more we had to staunch our tears and tend the flickering flame

Such wounds can't be forgotten, the damage lingered on

Until the healing advent of a second lusty son

For a while we knew calm sailing, being blessed by friendly tides

And a growing, blooming family, source of huge parental pride

A sojourn at the South Coast and a Caribbean tour

And a promise of the good life on a not too distant shore

Alas, it never happened, though heaven knows, I tried

This time when fate betrayed us, my dream it was that died

As with all our tribulations the reaction was the same

Bite the bullet, do the needful, hold the line – and tend the flame

So now as shadows lengthen and our sun begins to set

Though the way be long and weary, we're not quite finished yet

So we *will* go more a roving so late into the night

For the flame, so dearly tended, yet blossoms, clear and bright

But there's still one aching sorrow I can name without reserve

I never could provide you with the treasures you deserve

There's no more I can offer, though it's much less than your due

So all I have, my gift for words, I dedicate to you

My light, my life, my lover, my lodestar to the end

The simple truth; without you there would be no flame to tend.

CONTENTS

Milton Keynes UK
Ingram Content Group UK Ltd.
UKHW032154170724
445718UK00004B/76